AF428973

DEDICATION:

To Dad - a Brown Man Born
To "Chief" - a Fighting Quaker
To Emily - my favorite Greenie
With love and thanks,
"Rocky"

Lions, Tigers, and... Bulldogs?

An unofficial guide to the legends and lore of the Ivy League

by Matt Robinson
Penn, '96

Illustrated by **Jim Roldan**

Hi, I'm Ivy!

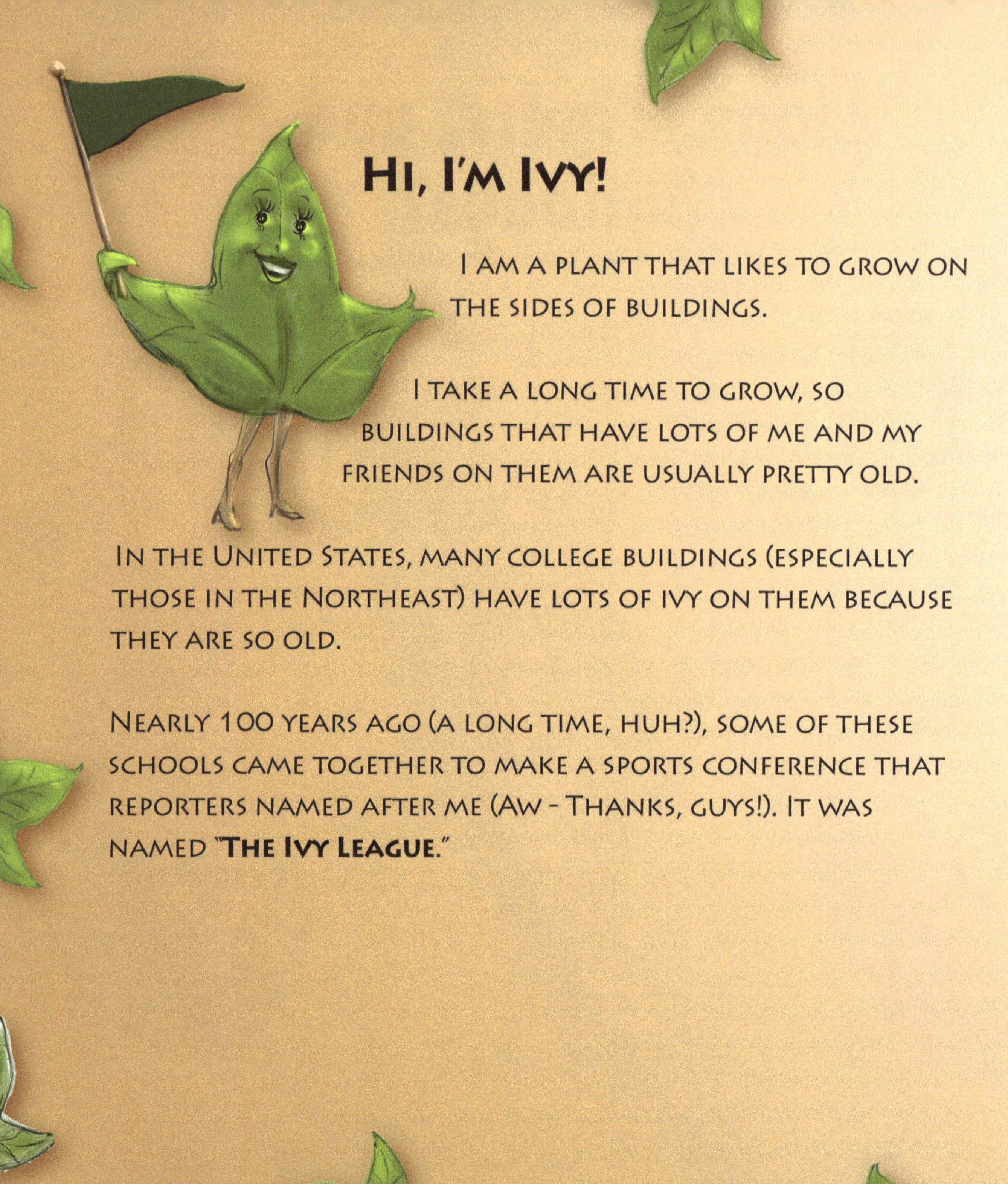

I AM A PLANT THAT LIKES TO GROW ON THE SIDES OF BUILDINGS.

I TAKE A LONG TIME TO GROW, SO BUILDINGS THAT HAVE LOTS OF ME AND MY FRIENDS ON THEM ARE USUALLY PRETTY OLD.

IN THE UNITED STATES, MANY COLLEGE BUILDINGS (ESPECIALLY THOSE IN THE NORTHEAST) HAVE LOTS OF IVY ON THEM BECAUSE THEY ARE SO OLD.

NEARLY 100 YEARS AGO (A LONG TIME, HUH?), SOME OF THESE SCHOOLS CAME TOGETHER TO MAKE A SPORTS CONFERENCE THAT REPORTERS NAMED AFTER ME (AW – THANKS, GUYS!). IT WAS NAMED **"THE IVY LEAGUE."**

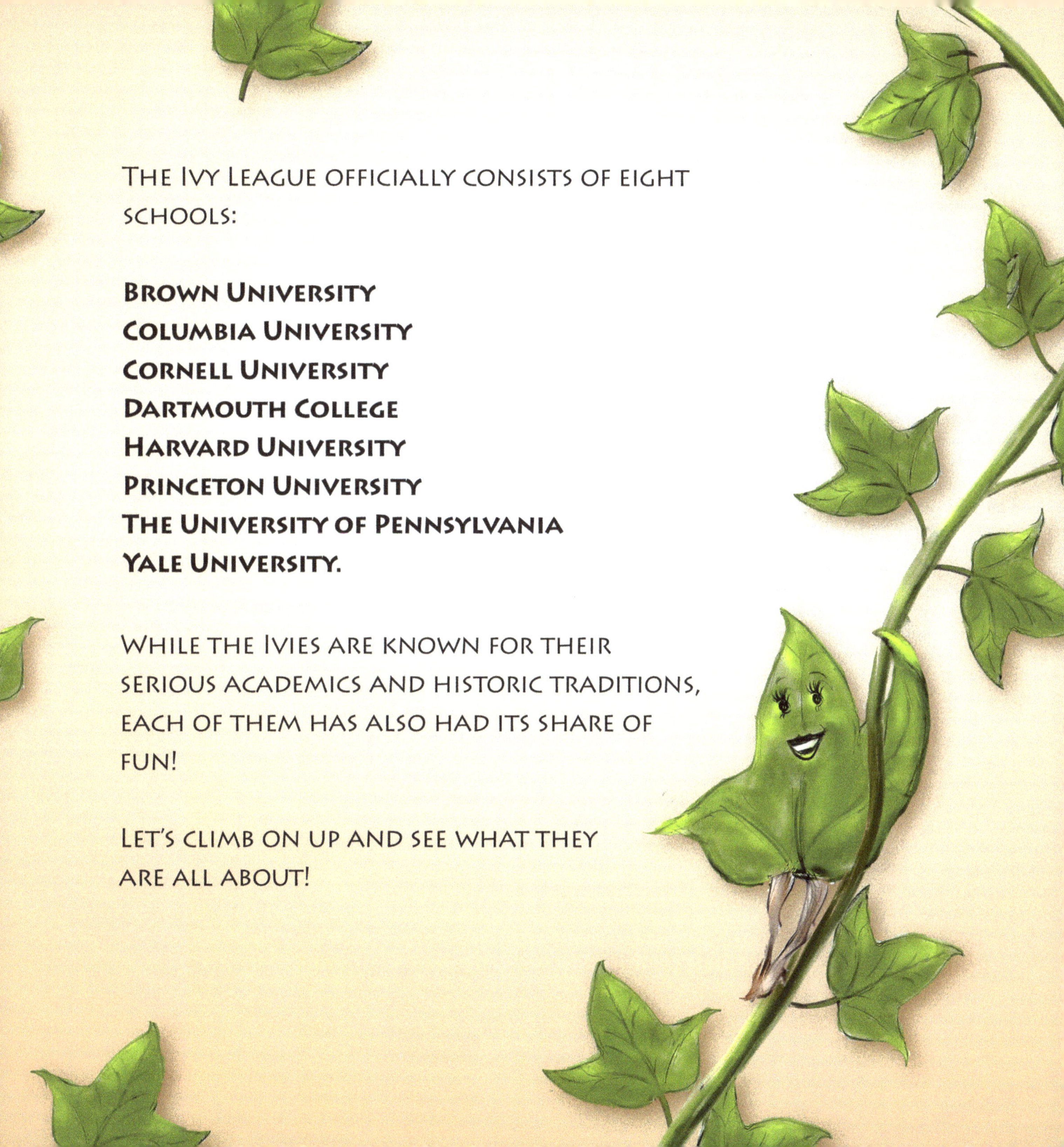

The Ivy League officially consists of eight schools:

Brown University
Columbia University
Cornell University
Dartmouth College
Harvard University
Princeton University
The University of Pennsylvania
Yale University.

While the Ivies are known for their serious academics and historic traditions, each of them has also had its share of fun!

Let's climb on up and see what they are all about!

The Ivy League

Historic Names:

The Rowing Association of American Colleges (1870)

Intercollegiate Rowing Association (1895)

Eastern Intercollegiate Basketball League (1902)

Important Dates:

1933 – Stanley Woodward of The *New York Herald Tribune* uses the term "Ivy colleges" in print to describe a group of America's oldest colleges.

1935 – AP Sports Editor Alan Gould uses the exact term "Ivy League" in a story.

1936 – Seven of the current members of the Ivy League RUN simultaneous editorials in their school newspapers calling for the creation of an athletic league. The editorials cite "common interests" among the schools as a reason for officially uniting in this way.

1945 – The presidents of eight schools sign the Ivy Group Agreement. It sets academic and athletic standards and states that an applicant's ability to play on a team would not influence their admission decision.

1954 – The NCAA forms a Division I athletic conference consisting of eight historic schools in the Northeast.

Fun Facts:

- Some think that the term "Ivy League" comes from the Roman numeral *IV* (four), as there were four schools (Dartmouth, Harvard, Princeton, Yale) in the original league.

- Ivy League schools are highly selective. Typically fewer than 10% of applicants are accepted each year.

- Ivy League schools enroll 4,000-14,000 students each year, making them larger than typical private liberal arts colleges, but smaller than most public state schools.

- The Ivy League consists of seven of the so-called "Colonial Colleges" that were created before the American Revolution. Of its current members, only Cornell is younger than the United States itself.

- Many of the Ivy League schools incorporate ivy in school traditions.

- The Ivy League has occasionally considered admitting other schools, including The United States Military Academy, the United States Naval Academy, Georgetown, Syracuse, and Northwestern.

- Many schools—including the Massachusetts Institute of Technology, Stanford University, The University of Chicago, and Duke University—are often considered as Ivy League "Plus" schools, or as the "Ivy" of the West (Stanford), South (Duke), etc.

- Similarly, some liberal arts colleges (e.g., Amherst, Williams) are often categorized as "Little Ivies" and some state schools (e.g., the University of Michigan) as "Public Ivies."

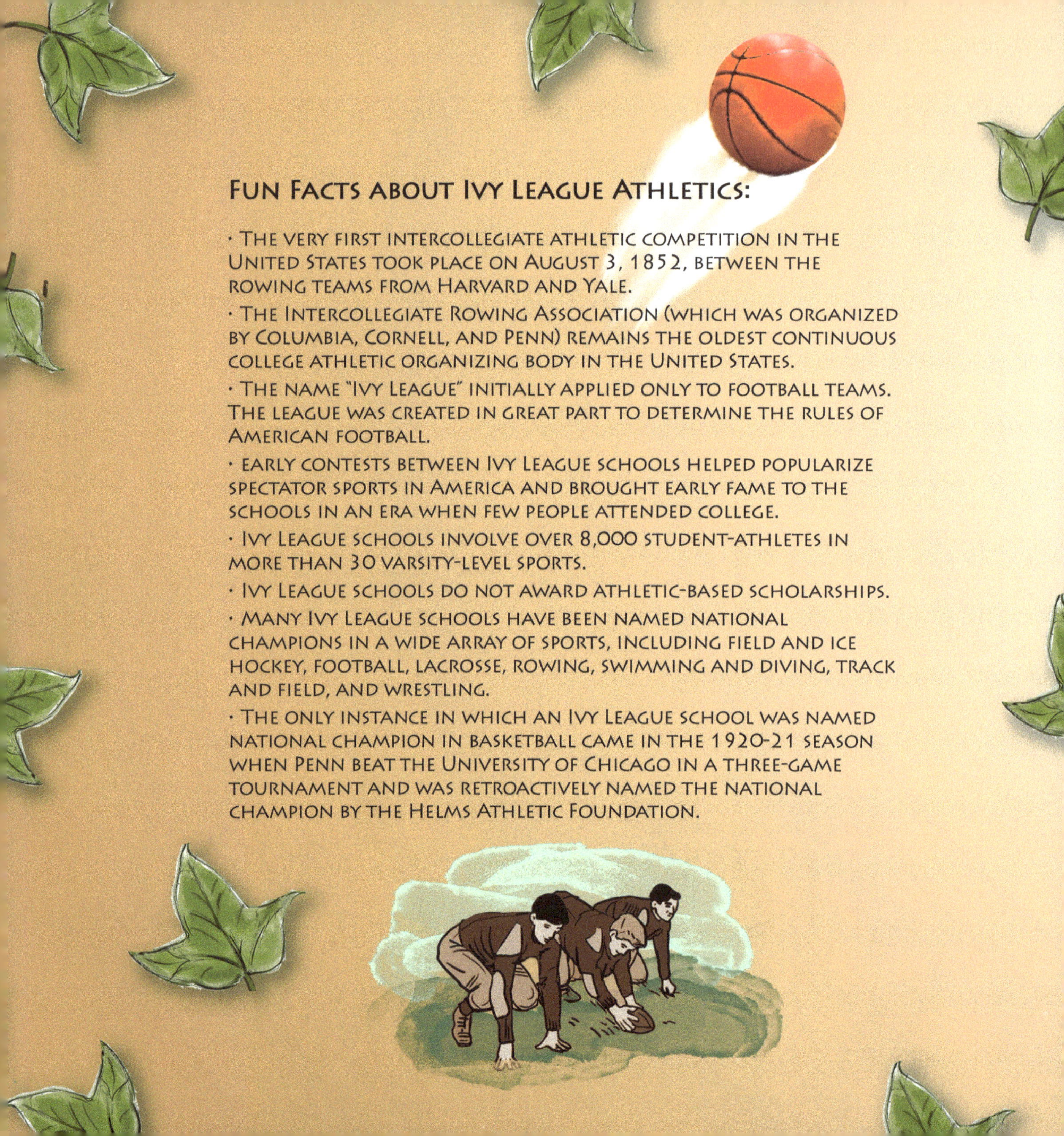

Fun Facts about Ivy League Athletics:

· The very first intercollegiate athletic competition in the United States took place on August 3, 1852, between the rowing teams from Harvard and Yale.

· The Intercollegiate Rowing Association (which was organized by Columbia, Cornell, and Penn) remains the oldest continuous college athletic organizing body in the United States.

· The name "Ivy League" initially applied only to football teams. The league was created in great part to determine the rules of American football.

· Early contests between Ivy League schools helped popularize spectator sports in America and brought early fame to the schools in an era when few people attended college.

· Ivy League schools involve over 8,000 student-athletes in more than 30 varsity-level sports.

· Ivy League schools do not award athletic-based scholarships.

· Many Ivy League schools have been named national champions in a wide array of sports, including field and ice hockey, football, lacrosse, rowing, swimming and diving, track and field, and wrestling.

· The only instance in which an Ivy League school was named national champion in basketball came in the 1920-21 season when Penn beat the University of Chicago in a three-game tournament and was retroactively named the national champion by the Helms Athletic Foundation.

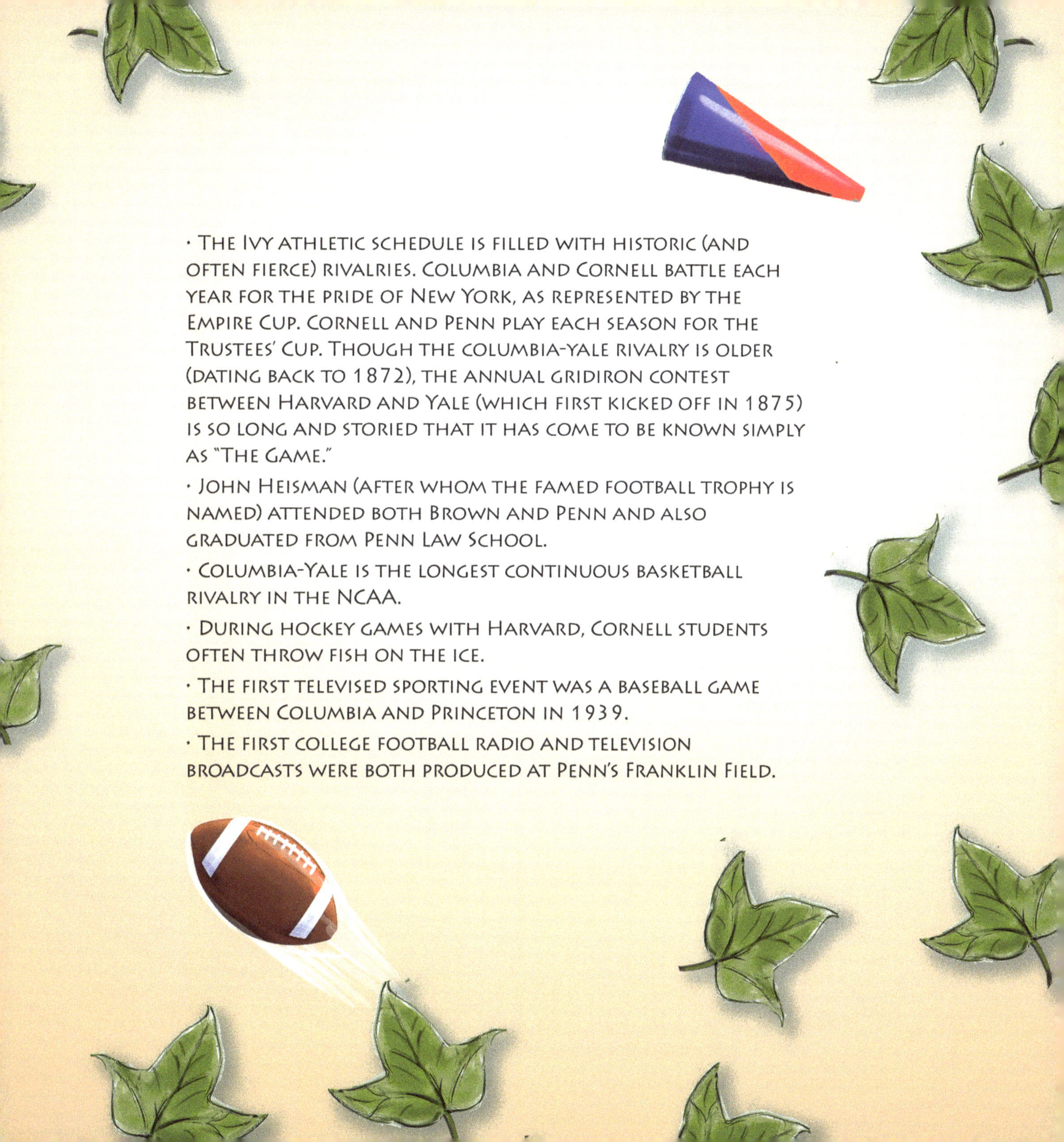

- The Ivy athletic schedule is filled with historic (and often fierce) rivalries. Columbia and Cornell battle each year for the pride of New York, as represented by the Empire Cup. Cornell and Penn play each season for the Trustees' Cup. Though the Columbia-Yale rivalry is older (dating back to 1872), the annual gridiron contest between Harvard and Yale (which first kicked off in 1875) is so long and storied that it has come to be known simply as "The Game."

- John Heisman (after whom the famed football trophy is named) attended both Brown and Penn and also graduated from Penn Law School.

- Columbia-Yale is the longest continuous basketball rivalry in the NCAA.

- During hockey games with Harvard, Cornell students often throw fish on the ice.

- The first televised sporting event was a baseball game between Columbia and Princeton in 1939.

- The first college football radio and television broadcasts were both produced at Penn's Franklin Field.

BROWN UNIVERSITY

LOCATION: PROVIDENCE, RI
ORIGINAL NAME: RHODE ISLAND COLLEGE (CHARTERED AS THE COLLEGE OR UNIVERSITY IN THE ENGLISH COLONY OF RHODE ISLAND AND PROVIDENCE PLANTATIONS, IN NEW ENGLAND, IN AMERICA)
DATE OF FOUNDING: 1764
MOTTO: *IN DEO SPERAMUS* (LATIN FOR "IN GOD WE HOPE")
MASCOT: THE BROWN BEAR

RHODE ISLAND COLLEGE WAS RENAMED BROWN WHEN NICHOLAS BROWN DONATED $5000 TO SUPPORT THE SCHOOL IN 1804. AT THE TIME TUITION WAS $5!

THE UNIVERSITY IS DIVIDED INTO TWO CAMPUSES: MAIN CAMPUS AND PEMBROKE, WHICH WAS ONCE THE CAMPUS FOR WOMEN.

BROWN UNIVERSITY WAS THE FIRST SCHOOL IN THE NATION TO ACCEPT STUDENTS OF ALL RELIGIOUS FAITHS.

THE TOP OF THE SCIENCES LIBRARY IS THE HIGHEST POINT IN PROVIDENCE. ITS 14-FLIGHT STAIRWELL IS COLOR-CODED ACCORDING TO THE pH SCALE.

VAN WICKLE GATES ARE OPENED ONLY TWICE EACH YEAR—ONCE TO LET NEW STUDENTS IN FOR CONVOCATION AND AGAIN TO LET GRADUATES OUT FOR COMMENCEMENT.

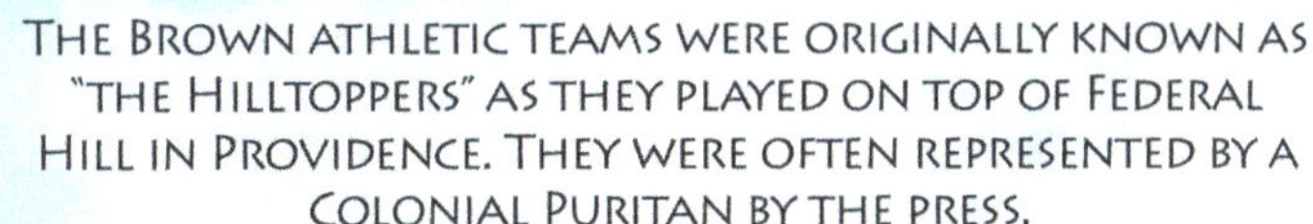

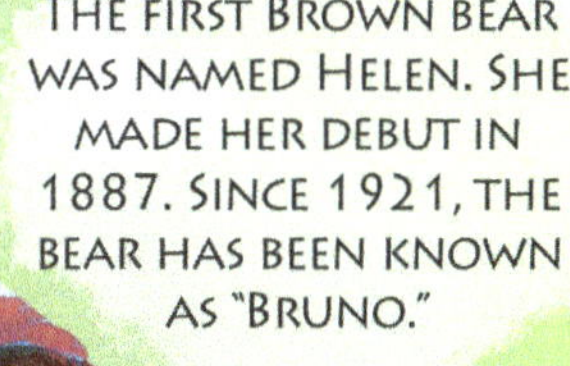

Started in 1824, Brown's Pacifica House (originally known as Franklin Society) is America's oldest secret student society.

The first Brown bear was named Helen. She made her debut in 1887. Since 1921, the bear has been known as "Bruno."

Brown's original mascot was a brown and white burro.

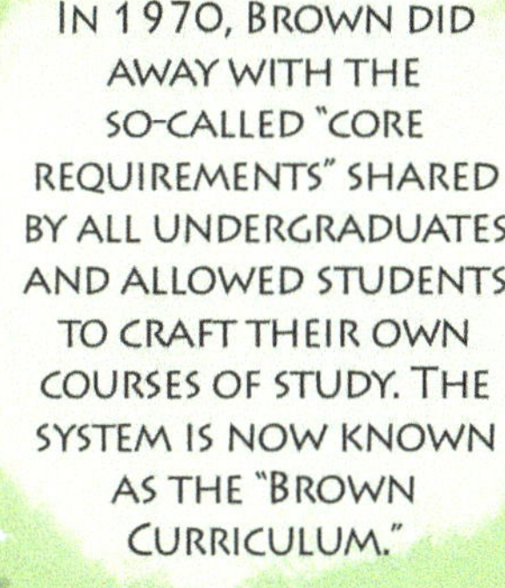

In 1970, Brown did away with the so-called "core requirements" shared by all undergraduates and allowed students to craft their own courses of study. The system is now known as the "Brown Curriculum."

LOCATION: NEW YORK CITY, NY
ORIGINAL NAME: KING'S COLLEGE
DATE OF FOUNDING: 1754
MOTTO: *IN LUMINE TUO VIDEBIMUS LUMEN*
(LATIN FOR "IN THY LIGHT SHALL WE SEE LIGHT")
MASCOT: ROAR-EE THE LION

CHARTERED BY KING GEORGE OF ENGLAND IN 1754, (APPARENTLY IN REACTION TO THE FOUNDING OF PRINCETON), THE SCHOOL WAS ORIGINALLY KNOWN AS KING'S COLLEGE AND STILL USES A CROWN AS A PROMINENT SYMBOL.

THE SCHOOL WAS RENAMED COLUMBIA UNIVERSITY AFTER THE AMERICAN REVOLUTION.

LOW MEMORIAL LIBRARY, WHICH WAS DESIGNED BY THE FIRM OF MCKIM, MEAD AND WHITE, IS FRONTED BY THE STATUE OF *ALMA MATER* BY DANIEL CHESTER FRENCH, WHO ALSO DESIGNED THE LINCOLN MEMORIAL AND THE (ALLEGED) JOHN HARVARD STATUE (SEE HARVARD).

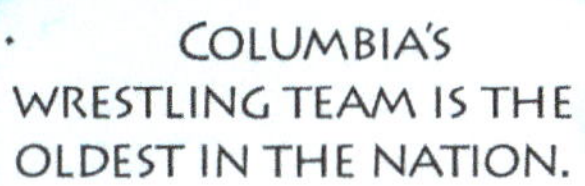

COLUMBIA CHOSE THE LION AS ITS MASCOT AS A REFERENCE TO THE SCHOOL'S "ROYAL" PAST.

THE LION IS NAMED "ROAR-EE" AFTER THE COLUMBIA FIGHT SONG, "ROAR, LION, ROAR."

IN 1934, COLUMBIA WON THE ROSE BOWL. BETWEEN 1983 AND 1988, COLUMBIA LOST 44 FOOTBALL GAMES IN A ROW.

COLUMBIA'S PUPIN HALL IS THE BIRTHPLACE OF FM RADIO AND THE LASER. IT WAS ALSO THE SITE OF IMPORTANT PARTS OF THE MANHATTAN PROJECT WHICH LED TO THE DEVELOPMENT OF THE ATOMIC BOMB.

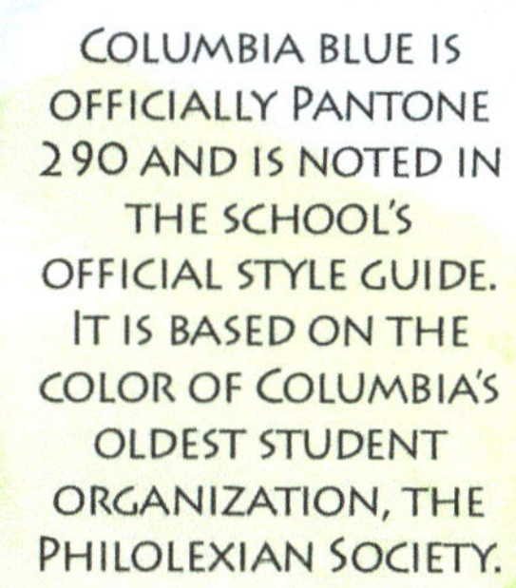

COLUMBIA BLUE IS OFFICIALLY PANTONE 290 AND IS NOTED IN THE SCHOOL'S OFFICIAL STYLE GUIDE. IT IS BASED ON THE COLOR OF COLUMBIA'S OLDEST STUDENT ORGANIZATION, THE PHILOLEXIAN SOCIETY.

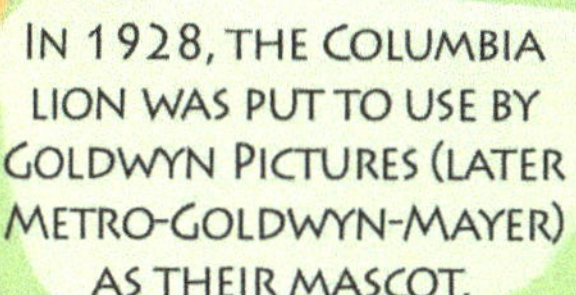

IN 1928, THE COLUMBIA LION WAS PUT TO USE BY GOLDWYN PICTURES (LATER METRO-GOLDWYN-MAYER) AS THEIR MASCOT.

Cornell University

Location: Ithaca, NY
Original Name: Cornell University
Date of Founding: 1865
Motto: "I would found an institution where any person can find instruction in any study."
– Ezra Cornell
Mascot: The Big Red (unofficially Touchdown, the Bear)

In 1868, Cornell's inaugural class of 412 students was the largest entering class in American history to that point.

Cornell awarded the world's first degree in journalism, the nation's first degree in veterinary medicine, and the first doctorates in electrical and industrial engineering

Cornell was among the first schools in the nation to reject racial and gender discrimination in its admissions policies.

The Johnson Museum of Art was designed by the firm of I.M. Pei and is considered among the nation's most important university museums.

Cornell's Big Red Marching Band is the only corps-style marching band in the Ivy League.

Cornell is home to the charter chapter of Alpha Phi Alpha, the first Greek-letter fraternity created by and for African-American students. Today, it has over 400 chapters that accept members of all ethnicities.

Cornell's colors (red and white) inspired the design of Campbell's soup cans.

ΑΦΑ

In 2017, Cornell partnered with the Technion in Israel to open a technical campus on Roosevelt Island in New York City.

Cornell Professor Robert C. Baker is credited with inventing the chicken nugget. He is a member of the American Poultry Hall of Fame.

Cornell also has a medical school campus in Qatar that represents the first American medical school outside of the United States.

DARTMOUTH COLLEGE

Location: Hanover, NH
Original Name: Dartmouth College
Date of Founding: 1769
Motto: *Vox clamantis in deserto* (Latin for "The voice of one crying out in the wilderness")
Mascot: The Dartmouth Big Green (unofficially a moose)

Dartmouth College was originally the collegiate department of Moor's Charity School, a secondary school started in 1754 by Dartmouth founder Eleazar Wheelock.

In 1937, Dartmouth was invited to the Rose Bowl, but declined, as would become Ivy League tradition.

Dartmouth College is actually a university! In fact, it has a number of famed graduate programs, including a medical school that was renamed for famous Dartmouth alumnus Theodore Geisel (a.k.a. "Dr. Seuss")

The Hopkins Center for the Arts was designed by Wallace K. Harrison, who later designed the similar-looking Lincoln Center in New York.

Dartmouth was apparently given the name "Big Green" because, when their team played the Harvard baseball team in 1866, that was the color the team wore. In the 1920's, many area newspapers referred to Dartmouth's teams as "The Indians" (allegedly in reference to the college's founding mission of educating what were then often referred to as American Indians), but this has been discouraged by the school.

Students can request songs to be played on the bells in Baker Tower. Among popular tunes are "Happy Birthday" and the themes from Indiana Jones, Jeopardy, and The Smurfs.

Dartmouth was the first university to create a mentoring program to provide undergraduate women opportunities to perform research with faculty in their fields of interest. It is called the Women in Science Project (WISP).

Founded in 1885, The Sphinx is the oldest continuously-operating all-male secret society in the country.

The film "Animal House" was written by (and allegedly based on) members of a fraternity at Dartmouth (though the movie was not filmed there).

Dartmouth has an Outing Club and its own ski mountain!

LOCATION: CAMBRIDGE, MA
ORIGINAL NAME: NEW COLLEGE
DATE OF FOUNDING: 1636
MOTTO: *VERITAS* (LATIN FOR "TRUTH")
MASCOT: THE HARVARD CRIMSON

HARVARD IS THE OLDEST CHARTERED CORPORATION IN THE UNITED STATES.

THE LAMPOON CASTLE IS THE HOME OF THE *HARVARD LAMPOON*, THE SATIRICAL PUBLICATION THAT LAUNCHED THE CAREERS OF SUCH WRITERS AS B. J. NOVAK, CONAN O'BRIEN, GEORGE PLIMPTON, GEORGE SANTAYANA, AND JOHN UPDIKE.

IN 1846, HARVARD MEDICAL SCHOOL PROFESSOR JOHN COLLINS WARREN DEMONSTRATED THE FIRST PUBLIC USE OF ETHER AS A SURGICAL ANESTHETIC AT MASSACHUSETTS GENERAL HOSPITAL.

HARVARD'S FIRST GRADUATING CLASS IN 1642 HAD NINE MEMBERS.

Harvard competes annually in hockey against Boston College, Boston University and Northeastern University in what is known as the "Beanpot" tournament. The winner receives a bronze pot of Boston baked beans.

Harvard's original mascot was known as "John the Orange Man" and was named for an actual produce seller in Harvard Square.

Harvard's financial endowment is the largest of any academic institution in the world.

Opened in 1903, Harvard Stadium was the first concrete stadium in the nation.

In 1879, Harvard opened the Harvard Annex (later Radcliffe College) for women to attend.

A statue in Harvard Yard is traditionally known as "The Statute of the Three Lies," as it does not depict John Harvard (the model was Sherman Hoar), as John Harvard did not actually found (or even attend) the school (rather, he was the first major benefactor, donating 400 books from his personal library), and as the date of the school's founding noted on the statue is 1638 (the school was officially created in 1636).

Princeton University

LOCATION: Princeton, NJ
ORIGINAL NAME: College of New Jersey
DATE OF FOUNDING: 1746
MOTTO: *Dei sub numine viget*
(Latin for "Under the Protection of God She Flourishes")
MASCOT: The Princeton Tiger

Princeton's "informal" motto is, "Princeton, in the Nation's Service and in the Service of Humanity."

On November 19, 1969, Princeton alumnus Charles "Pete" Conrad brought a Princeton flag to the moon.

In 1774, Princeton was referred to by then president John Witherspoon as a "campus" (Latin for "field"), marking the first recorded usage of this now common term.

The Continental Congress met in Nassau Hall, which served as the capitol of the United States for about five months in 1783.

In 1969, statues of male and female tigers were commissioned for the Princeton campus to mark the first year of coeducation.

Princeton had a United States warship named for it in 1843. There is also an asteroid and a glacier named for the school.

Instead of fraternities and sororities (which are not officially recognized), Princeton offers eating clubs as places of dining and social gathering.

In 1869, the first American intercollegiate football game was played between Princeton and Rutgers.

Princeton is credited with being the home of the first athletic cheer.

Princeton's American Whig-Cliosophic Society is one of the oldest collegiate political, literary, and debating groups in the country.

UNIVERSITY OF PENNSYLVANIA

LOCATION: PHILADELPHIA, PA
ORIGINAL NAME:
ACADEMY AND CHARITABLE SCHOOL IN THE PROVINCE OF PENNSYLVANIA.
DATE OF FOUNDING: 1740
MOTTO: *LEGES SINE MORIBUS VANAE*
(LATIN FOR "LAWS WITHOUT MORALS ARE USELESS")
MASCOT: (FIGHTING) QUAKERS

PENN IS THE FIRST OFFICIAL "UNIVERSITY" IN THE UNITED STATES. PENN MEDICAL SCHOOL (FOUNDED IN 1765) WAS THE FIRST SCHOOL IN THE NATION TO OFFER PROFESSIONAL EDUCATION. WHARTON (FOUNDED IN 1881) IS THE FIRST COLLEGIATE BUSINESS SCHOOL IN THE UNITED STATES.

IN 1994, DR. JUDITH RODIN BECAME THE FIRST PERMANENT FEMALE PRESIDENT OF AN IVY LEAGUE UNIVERSITY.

THE ORIGINAL COLLEGE HALL WAS THE SITE OF MEETINGS BY THE CONTINENTAL CONGRESS IN 1775. THE CURRENT VERSION HAS ALSO BEEN CLAIMED AS THE INSPIRATION FOR THE ADDAMS FAMILY'S HOME, AS DESIGNED BY PENN ALUM CHARLES ADDAMS.

PENN'S COLORS – RED AND BLUE – ARE INTENDED TO BE THE SAME AS THOSE USED BY THE UNITED STATES GOVERNMENT FOR ITS OFFICIAL FLAGS.

Despite its mascot, Penn is not a Quaker institution and, in fact, has no affiliation to any religion or belief.

Penn students traditionally throw toast on the football field while singing, "Drink a Highball," which concludes with the lyric, "Here's a toast to Dear Old Penn."

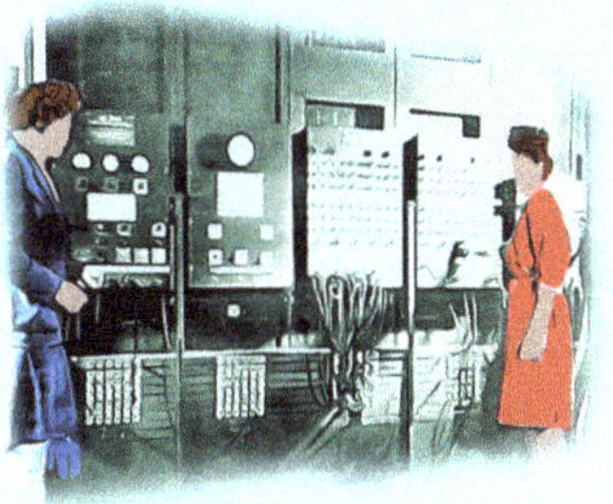

The first general-purpose electronic computer (ENIAC) was developed in 1946 at the Moore School of Electrical Engineering.

Opened in 1895, Franklin Field is the oldest double-decker stadium and oldest football stadium in the country. It is also home to the Penn Relays, the longest uninterrupted track meet in the country.

Penn's basketball team also plays in the "Big Five," a group of Philadelphia universities that also includes LaSalle, St. Joseph's, Temple, and Villanova. All Penn home games are played in the Palestra, which is commonly known as "The Cathedral of College Basketball."

In 1980, Franklin Field hosted the Liberty Bell Classic, a competition among 29 countries who were boycotting the Olympic Games in Russia.

YALE UNIVERSITY

LOCATION: NEW HAVEN, CT
ORIGINAL NAME: COLLEGIATE SCHOOL
DATE OF FOUNDING: 1701
MOTTO: *LUX ET VERITAS*
(LATIN FOR "LIGHT AND TRUTH")
MASCOT: THE YALE BULLDOG

THE NAME OF THE SCHOOL WAS CHANGED TO YALE IN 1718 WHEN ELIHU YALE – GOVERNOR OF THE EAST INDIA TRADING COMPANY – DONATED A CRATE OF GOODS TO HELP THE STRUGGLING INSTITUTION CONTINUE TO OPERATE.

YALE WAS FOUNDED BY ALUMNI FROM HARVARD (WHICH MAY EXPLAIN THE FIERCE RIVALRY BETWEEN THE SCHOOLS).

INGALLS RINK IS COMMONLY REFERRED TO AS "THE WHALE" THANKS TO ITS DESIGN BY YALE-TRAINED ARCHITECT EERO SAARINEN.

FOUNDED IN 1878, THE *YALE DAILY NEWS* IS THE OLDEST COLLEGE DAILY NEWSPAPER STILL IN EXISTENCE.

ESTABLISHED IN 1909, YALE'S FAMED A CAPPELLA SINGING GROUP THE WHIFFENPOOFS IS THE NATION'S OLDEST SUCH ORGANIZATION.

YALE IS KNOWN FOR ITS "SECRET" SOCIETIES, SUCH AS SKULL AND BONES, WHICH HAS INCLUDED PRESIDENTS WILLIAM HOWARD TAFT, GEORGE H. W. BUSH AND GEORGE W. BUSH AMONG ITS MEMBERS.

YALE'S MASCOT—THE BULLDOG NAMED "HANDSOME DAN"— IS THE FIRST LIVE MASCOT IN AMERICAN HISTORY.

THE ORIGINAL DAN WON FIRST PRIZE AT THE WESTMINSTER DOG SHOW. DAN II WAS KIDNAPPED BY HARVARD STUDENTS.

YALE WAS ORIGINALLY INTENDED TO BE A SCHOOL FOR CLERGY.

YALE FOOTBALL COACH WALTER CAMP, POPULARLY KNOWN AS THE "FATHER" OF AMERICAN FOOTBALL, IS CREDITED WITH DEVELOPING SUCH INNOVATIONS AS THE LINE OF SCRIMMAGE AND A SYSTEM OF DOWNS. HE WAS THE ALL-TIME LEADER IN WINNING PERCENTAGE IN COLLEGE FOOTBALL IN THE 20TH CENTURY.

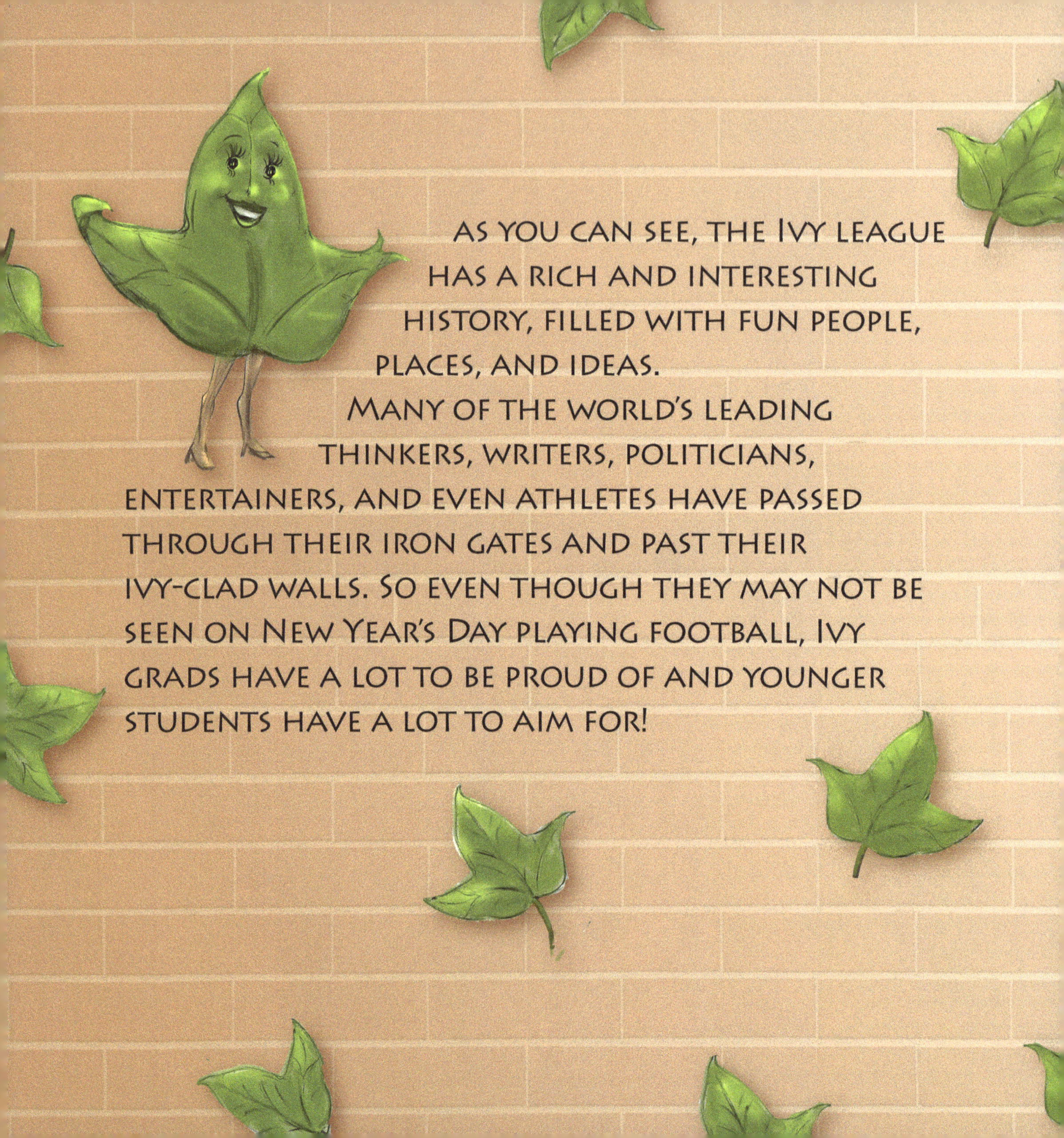

As you can see, the Ivy League
has a rich and interesting
history, filled with fun people,
places, and ideas.
Many of the world's leading
thinkers, writers, politicians,
entertainers, and even athletes have passed
through their iron gates and past their
ivy-clad walls. So even though they may not be
seen on New Year's Day playing football, Ivy
grads have a lot to be proud of and younger
students have a lot to aim for!

I HOPE TO SEE YOU AROUND CAMPUS
SOON. BE SURE TO LOOK FOR ME
CLIMBING THE WALLS LIKE I ALWAYS DO.

BYE-BYE!